Buzzing Bees:
Discovering Odd Numbers

by Amanda Doering Tourville

illustrated by Sharon Holm

Content Consultant: Paula J. Maida, PhD, and Terry Sinko, Instructional Support Teacher

magic
wagon

Published by Magic Wagon, a division of the ABDO Publishing Group, 8000 West 78th Street, Edina, Minnesota, 55439. Copyright © 2009 by Abdo Consulting Group, Inc. International copyrights reserved in all countries. All rights reserved. No part of this book may be reproduced in any form without written permission from the publisher.

Printed in the United States.

Text by Amanda Doering Tourville
Illustrations by Sharon Holm
Edited by Patricia Stockland
Interior layout and design by Becky Daum
Cover design by Becky Daum

Library of Congress Cataloging-in-Publication Data

Tourville, Amanda Doering, 1980–
  Buzzing bees : discovering odd numbers / by Amanda Doering Tourville ; illustrated by Sharon Holm.
      p. cm. — (Count the critters)
  ISBN 978-1-60270-262-2
  1. Counting—Juvenile literature. 2. Numbers, Prime—Juvenile literature. 3. Bees—Juvenile literature.
I. Holm, Sharon Lane, ill. II. Title.
  QA113.T684 2009
  513.2'11—dc22

                              2008001618

Odd numbers cannot be evenly divided into groups of two. See what odd numbers look like as you read about the interesting lives of honeybees.

Thousands of honeybees live together in a hive. One queen bee lays eggs. One is an odd number.

Thousands of honeybees live together in a hive. Three bees cool down the hive by fanning their wings. The three bees try to form groups of two, but one bee is left over. Three is an odd number.

Thousands of honeybees live together in a hive. Five bees feed the queen while she lays eggs. The five bees try to form groups of two, but one bee is left over. Five is an odd number.

Thousands of honeybees live together in a hive. Seven bees make a honeycomb to store honey and eggs. The seven bees try to form groups of two, but one bee is left over. Seven is an odd number.

Thousands of honeybees live together in a hive. Nine bees collect pollen from flowers. The nine bees try to form groups of two, but one bee is left over. Nine is an odd number.

Thousands of honeybees live together in a hive. Eleven bees remove nectar from flowers and bring it to the hive.

The eleven bees try to form groups
of two, but one bee is left over.
Eleven is an odd number.

Thousands of honeybees live together in a hive. Thirteen bees put nectar into honeycomb cells to make honey. The thirteen bees try to form groups of two, but one bee is left over. Thirteen is an odd number.

Thousands of honeybees live together in a hive. Fifteen bees feed baby bees in their honeycomb cells. The fifteen bees try to form groups of two, but one bee is left over. Fifteen is an odd number.

Thousands of honeybees live together in a hive. Seventeen bees guard the hive and will sting animals that come too close.

buzz-buzz

The seventeen bees try to form groups of two, but one bee is left over. Seventeen is an odd number.

buzz-buzz

buzz

Thousands of honeybees live together in a hive. Nineteen bees scout out a new place to build a hive. The nineteen bees try to form groups of two, but one bee is left over. Nineteen is an odd number.

buzz-buzz

buzz-buzz

Words to Know

hive—a home for bees.

honeycomb—a wax structure made by honeybees that holds honey and honeybee eggs.

nectar—a sweet liquid made by flowers; nectar can be made into honey.

pollen—a dusty substance made by flowers.

Web Sites

To learn more about odd numbers, visit ABDO Publishing Company on the World Wide Web at **www.abdopublishing.com**. Web sites about counting are featured on our Book Links page. These links are routinely monitored and updated to provide the most current information available.

1 2 3 4 5 6 7 8 9 10 11 12 13 14 15 16 17 18 19